A Friend Like You

Kettle's on, cups are waiting~ favorite chairs anticipating. No matter what I have to do~ my friend, there's always time for you.

D. Morgan

HARVEST HOUSE PUBLISHERS
EUGENE, OREGON 97402

To My Friend

With Love

Especially for you

With kind and loving thoughts

Friendship is neither a formality nor a mode; it is rather a life.

DAVID GRAYSON

Some there are can entertain me when the skies are fair,

Others cheer me when I'm gloomy by the smile they wear,

But with one I'm always happy, under cloudy skies or blue;

Need I tell you what the world knows, that that one is you.

You can change the rain to dewdrops, paint the clouds with gold,

Make the rainbow span the heaven that late storms foretold,

Scatter fragrance on the breezes that around me float,

Make the rivers flow with laughter, tune the songbird's throat.

'Tis the magic of true friendship soothes or heals life's ills,

Gives new life to weary spirits, nerves our flagging wills,

Helps us over dangerous passes on life's rocky way,

Broadcasts music on our midnight, heralds the coming day.

ROSALINA COWMAN

*Knowing you*
*are somewhere,*
*near or far,*
*means*
*I'm never, ever*
*totally alone.*

MARION GARRETTY

I will always love you ~ and want to be your friend

No matter where you've been... No matter where you're going ~

D. Morgan © 1991

Happiness is in the comfortable companionship of friends.

D. Morgan © 1992

"Stay" is a charming word

in a friend's vocabulary.

LOUISA MAY ALCOTT

Friendship...is a union of spirits,

a marriage of hearts,

and the bond thereto virtue.

WILLIAM PENN

Friendships are the best books

in the library of life.

WALLACE RICE

PAM BROWN

The way may be long and winding Up

D. Morgan © 1995

The ornament of a house
is the friends

ill against the wind.

But never too far to travel...

...to reach the home of a friend.

who frequent it.

*Ralph Waldo Emerson*

# The Friendship Chain

A friendship chain has many links
Connected one by one,
And through the length and breadth of it
Electric currents run.
Some links are made of solid gold
Of real intrinsic worth,
And these are treasured as the best
Of any on the earth.

And some are made of silver bright
Of sterling merit pure,
And valued well, because they will
Throughout all time endure.
Still others seeming naught but lead
Of dull and homely hue,
Have iron hearts, that ever prove
To be both good and true.

And many are the links on links
Of some material plain,
That worthy are to hold a place
In this true friendship chain.
For when life's waves by troubles tossed
Dash wild upon the shore,
They hold the frail bark anchored well
Until the storm is o'er.

Come wind or calm, come joy or woe,
Come dull or pleasant weather,
The links retain the same strong hold
That keeps the chain together.
For if perchance, through lapse of years
Some links may broken be,
The chain will never break, because
They hold invisibly.

JOSEPHINE CURRIER

*It* isn't so much

what's on the table that matters

as what's on the chairs.

W. S. GILBERT

*on dining with friends*

*If* I could keep one Friend alone—

From all the friends I knew...

...It would

Be

You.

D. MORGAN

Kettle's on, cups are waiting~ favorite chairs anticipating. No matter what I have to do~ my friend, there's always time for you.

There'll be no goodbyes for us, my very special friend. I wish you happy, safe and well, until ...... we meet again.

D. Morgan © 1994

*D*ear friend,

I pray that you may enjoy good health

and that all may go well with you,

even as your soul is getting along well.

THE BOOK OF 3 JOHN

*T*hink where man's glory most begins and ends,

And say my glory was I had such friends.

WILLIAM BUTLER YEATS

*I*f we would build on a sure foundation in friendship,

we must love friends for their sake rather than for our own.

CHARLOTTE BRONTË

A friendship can weather most things and thrive in thin soil, but it needs just a little mulch of letters and phone calls and small, silly presents every so often–just to save it from drying out completely.

PAM BROWN

D. Morgan © 1992

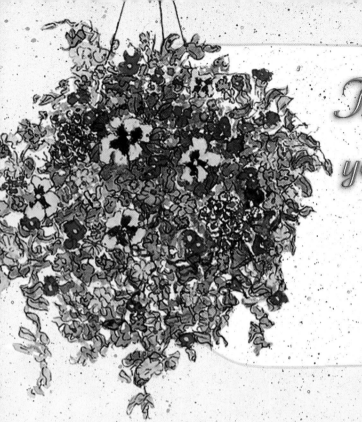

Treat your friends as
you do your pictures,
and place them
in their best light.

JENNIE JEROME CHURCHILL

A true friend is someone who
thinks that you are a good egg
even though he knows that
you are slightly cracked.

BERNARD MELTZER

Time changes many things... But not the joy your friendship brings.

© Morgan © 1996

Perhaps we'll share our tears and laughter,

and be friends forever after.

At my table, sit with me, I'll pour your coffee or some tea.

D. Morgan © 1994

*The* glory of friendship

is not the outstretched hand,

nor the kindly smile,

nor the joy of companionship;

it is the spiritual inspiration that

comes to one when he discovers

that someone else believes in him

and is willing to trust him.

RALPH WALDO EMERSON

*...and the pleasantness of one's friend springs from his earnest counsel.*

THE BOOK OF PROVERBS

*Dear Friends, let us love one another...*

THE BOOK OF 1 JOHN

## A Loyal Friend

Ain't it good when life seems dreary

And your hopes about to end,

Just to feel the handclasp cheery

Of a fine and loyal friend?

Ain't it fine when things are going

Topsy-turvy and askew,

To discover someone showing

Good old-fashioned faith in you?

EDGAR GUEST

My coat and I live comfortably together.

It has assumed all my wrinkles, does not

hurt me anywhere, has molded itself on my

deformities, and is complacent to all my

movements, and I only feel its presence because

it keeps me warm. Old coats and

old friends are the same thing.

VICTOR HUGO

I have not stopped giving thanks for you,
remembering you in my prayers.
THE BOOK OF EPHESIANS

You're a treasure when I'm happy ~ a comfort when I'm blue ~ there is no better friend in all the world ..... than you.

D. Morgan ©1993

I want a warm and faithful friend,

To cheer the adverse hour;

Who ne'er to flatter will descend,

Not bend the knee to power.

A friend to chide me when I'm wrong,

My inmost soul to see;

And that my friendship prove as strong

To him as his to me.

JOHN QUINCY ADAMS

D. Morgan ©1992

I have learned that to have a good friend is t
change of paym
I have learned that to ha
love th
ment. I hav
od's gifts.
change
the pur
ve tha
ave a good
's gi
ve learned
e pur
payment. I
a good
s no exc
e learned th
it is
hange of payment.
D. Morgan © 1996

$\mathcal{W}$e are all travelers in

what John Bunyan calls the wilderness

of this world—and the best that we find in our

travels is an honest friend. He is a fortunate voyager who finds

many. We travel, indeed, to find them. They are the end reward of life.

ROBERT LOUIS STEVENSON

$\mathcal{W}$e are sometimes made aware of a kindness long passed, and realize

that there have been times when our friends' thoughts of us were of

so pure and lofty a character that they passed over us like the

winds of heaven unnoticed; when they treat us not as

what we were, but as what we aspire to be.

HENRY DAVID THOREAU

FARMER

She threw her arms

around the Lion's neck and kissed him,

patting his big head tenderly. Then she kissed the

Tin Woodsman...she hugged the soft, stuffed body of

the Scarecrow in her arms instead of kissing his painted

face, and found she was crying herself at this sorrowful

parting from her loving comrades.

...Dorothy now took Toto up solemnly in her arms, and

having said one last good-bye she clapped the heels

of her shoes together three times, saying,

"Take me home to Aunt Em!"

L. FRANK BAUM
*The Wizard of Oz*

*Friendship only is,*
*indeed, genuine when*
*two friends,*
*without speaking*
*a word to each other,*
*can nevertheless*
*find happiness in*
*being together.*

GEORGE EBERS

We are kindred spirits.

D. Morgan© 1994

I can't imagine.....

.....in all the world ~
a better
friend
than
you.

D. Morgan ©1990

*A* friend is dearer than the

light of heaven, for it would

be better for us that

the sun were extinguished than

that we should be without friends.

SAINT CHYSOSTOM

*One's friends are that part of the human race with which one can be human.*

GEORGE SANTAYANA

D. Morgan © 1993

# Mizpah

$\mathcal{G}$o thou thy way, and I go mine;

Apart, yet not afar;

Only a thin veil hangs between

The pathways where we are.

And "God keep watch 'tween thee and me."

This is my prayer,

He looks thy way, He looketh mine,

And keeps us near.

JULIA A. BAKER

*In* friendship...we think we have chosen our peers. In reality, a few years of difference in the date of our births, a few more miles between certain houses, the choice of one university instead of another, posting to different regiments, the accident of a topic being raised or not raised at a first meeting—any of these chances might have kept us apart. But...there are, strictly speaking, no chances. A secret Master of Ceremonies has been at work...The Friendship is not a reward for our discrimination and good taste in finding one another out. It is the instrument by which God reveals to each the beauties of all others. They are no greater than the beauties of a thousand other men; by Friendship God opens our eyes to them. They are, like all beauties, derived from Him, and then, in a good Friendship, increased by time through the Friendship itself, so that it is His instrument for creation as well as for revealing.

C. S. Lewis
*The Four Loves*

D. Morgan © 1989

Seldom an evening has ended

Rarely a new
day begins
That I don't think
about you ~
Good times ~
True loves ~
Old
Friends.

D. Morgan © 1993

You're such a nice person,
No matter the season,
That you're in my thoughts
Without any reason.
You're friendly and cheerful
Each day of the year,
And folks always smile
Whenever you're near.
During the day
I quite often find
A kind word or deed
Brings you to my mind.
You're such a nice person
And I'd like to say
That just thinking of you
Brings pleasure my way!

PATRICIA MANGEAU

I wish you a fire to warm you in win
A cool breeze on a summer day......

May your journey
Through life
Be long
And Downhil

_Friendships begun_

_in this world_

_will be taken up again,_

_never to be broken off._

SAINT FRANCIS DE SALES

_A_ friend loves at all times.

THE BOOK OF PROVERBS

he Way.

D. Morgan © 1991

Friends we were ~ Friends we are ~

Friends we were

D. Morgan © 1996

Friends we'll always be.

*Hearts are linked*

*to hearts by God. The friend on*

*whose fidelity you can count, whose success*

*in life flushes your cheek with honest satisfaction,*

*whose triumphant career you have traced and read with a*

*heart throbbing almost as if it were a thing alive,*

*for whose honor you would answer as for your*

*own—that friend, given to you by*

*circumstances over which you*

*have no control, was*

*God's own gift.*

FREDERIC WILLIAM ROBERTSON

Thank you.....

For being someone special.